LIFE SUPPORT

The Student's Survival Guide To Help
Turn Troubles into Triumphs

MELQAAM SHAW

TO: _____

FROM: _Melqaam C. Shaw_____

Life Support

Book Design & Layout: Kantis Simmons
The SIMAKAN GROUP

Printed in the United States of America

TABLE OF CONTENTS

FOREWORD

Faith

'Be strong and courageous. Do not be terrified because of them, for the Lord your God goes with you; He will never leave you nor forsake you.' Deuteronomy 31:6

Will he live? Will he die? Who did it? Why? These questions popped into my head, but the scripture kept overriding all thoughts, questions, cries, screaming, worrying, anxiety, and anything else that you can think of. When I received the call one early morning (perhaps around 4:00AM), I clung to God. I held on to my faith. No one knows the day, the hour or the time that we will depart from this earth. However, we certainly know that we can embrace every single moment, be present, be grateful, and know that He is God.

My family and I left Washington, DC and headed to Myrtle Beach, SC in the midst of a storm (literally and figuratively). I remember getting out of the car and removing branches from the middle of the road that were there due to severe wind, rain, thunder and lightening. We were trying to get to the hospital and touch my brother's heart (if it was still beating) and hold his hands (whether they were warm or cold). We knew that he was on life support. We knew that he was in critical condition and uncertain if he'd live. We knew that even if he lived, there was a possibility of him not being able to swallow and properly eat. There was a possibility that he wouldn't be able to see. This was due to the damage and severity of the incident.

4

When he was released from the hospital, we were told that the recovery and healing would be lengthy. The surgeons also set up several appointments for multiple specialists and therapists. Without question, I requested leave from my job to help with the process. I remember bathing my adult brother as if he was again an infant. It wasn't pleasant, but perhaps as the saying goes, 'anything that comes to easily' is not worth it. It was worth it to support. It was worth it to have 'faith of a mustard seed'. It was worth it to have faith of the seen and unseen – insurmountable. It was worth it to have faith 'with work' in order for him to live. Otherwise, he'd be physically, emotionally, and mentally dead. So I'm grateful for God's handy work and miracles through people (right here on earth).

Faith, belief

I knew that if God gave him another chance, he'd live to tell his story and would live 'on purpose' for the rest of his life. I believe that whatever obstacles we face, it makes us stronger. It builds our resiliency, tenacity, and our faith. It makes us wiser. It helps us to grow.

Growing up, there were many challenges, but we did not give up. We believed in God, had support from our family and community, and had faith and hope that has propelled us into productive and positive members of society. We live to tell our stories and help someone else. We live to say that anything is indeed possible. We live to share what God has given us 'Life' and to live it joyfully, peacefully, and abundantly.

Light, Love, Energy,

Octavia Shaw-Williams
September 18, 2018

5

Introduction

1. If you are a high school student, I created this book so you can know why your life matters.

2. If you are a college student, I created this book so you can learn how to navigate your life.

3. If you are a single parent, I created this book so you can raise responsible children.

4. If you have experienced trauma, tragedy, or failure, I created this book so that you can believe life-fulfillment is possible for you.

5. I created this book for you, so you can turn your past troubles into triumph.

6. I created this book to show how a near death experience taught me how to live again.

7. I created this book so that dead dreams can live again.

Chapter 1

I Had a Dream

Have you ever had a dream? A dream so big that it scares you? A dream that turns your stomach upside down! A dream so enormous, that it exposes your fears. I have! For years, I had visions of telling my story on stages all over the world.

There I was, in an all-white suit with white dress shoes. The kind of shoes that do not have shoe strings; ones you slip on and wear with no socks. The stage was gigantic and I was in the zone. The spotlight was on me and I could just feel sixty-thousand eyes piercing me, as they were sitting on the edge of their seats, waiting for me to finish my story. When I finished, they were in tears and they all wanted a chance to speak with me. It was one of the best feelings of my life. That event was the event that changed my life, financially and spiritually. Well, that day still has yet to arrive. It was just a dream!

What do you do when God gives you a dream that is life changing? What do you do, day in and day out, while patiently awaiting that day, but it never finds you? How do you live, knowing that you have so much potential, yet no outlet to showcase that greatness? These are all questions that I ask myself, daily. We hear people say, "Walk by faith and not by sight", but what do you do when you are at a point where you can no longer mentally and spiritually walk? What do you do when you have waited twenty-seven years for God to fulfill that dream? Then the thought hits you. What if that dream is never fulfilled?

It was a beautiful day in Myrtle Beach, South Carolina. The day that changed my life. It was August 21, 2011, a day I will cherish forever. It was the day before my Junior year of college.

Ring, ring…

"What's good my dawg?"

"Man, we going in tonight! You down?"

"Hell yeah! Say no more, all the girls coming back tonight."

"Word, we going to hit that house party and turn up!"

"Aight say no more fam. One!"

"One!"

My best friend, Terrell, and I always had a plan of action when it came to having fun and partying. We took pride in being the life of the party everywhere we went.

We pulled up to the house party, walked in, sparked a blunt or two, and popped a bottle or two. Ten minutes into the party, I got my first text message from one of my girls.

"Hey Black, I'm at Broadway. Where are you?

"I'm here, too", I lied.

I told Terrell that I was heading out and I suggested that he came with me, if he wanted to have a good night. He told me "no" because he finally had the chance to invest some quality time with a girl he had been working on for about three weeks. I did not blame him. She was gorgeous and new. Nothing like new.

In life, we are going to be challenged with many opportunities that will help us grow, whether we want to grow or not. The decision I made, in that split moment, would nearly cost me my life. Darn it - it did! Are the decisions that you are making now, costing you your life in the future... I learned that day to never make permanent decisions based on temporary feelings.

Write down what challenges you have encountered, that you still deal with today, and why those challenges currently bother you.

_____

_____

_____

_____

_____

_____

_____

_____

Beep! Beep! Beep! These are the sounds that I will never forget. When I looked up, there was Terrell, standing over me, in tears.

"He's awake", someone yelled.

"Mr. Shaw, Mr. Shaw, do you know where you are? You are in the Intensive Care Unit at Grand Strand Hospital."

I locked eyes with Terrell and all of my friends who were there. They stepped to the side and this little woman stepped up. It was my mother. Her eyes were filled with tears as she grabbed my hand and squeezed it. I tried my best to talk but for some reason I could not.

I could hear a loud noise and it sounded as if something was pumping air into my body, and it was. It was pumping air into me. The doctors had placed me in an induced coma, as a last resort, hoping that it would save my life. Honestly, I cannot describe what it felt like because I had no feelings. I just remember hearing people come in and out of my hospital room. I remained in the Intensive Care Unit for three and a half days, clinging to life. My total stay was seven days. Those were the longest seven days of my life.

I had to learn how to stand on my own, again. I had to let my mom and family members clean me up, after I used the restroom. I lost weight. I watched myself go into this dark place. On top of that, my girlfriend had to witness it all. Both of them! Yes, you read it right.

Imagine that you are on life support and you have two girlfriends who are holding hands and praying for you, along with one of their mothers. Literally, crying together, sitting in your room together, and both are praying for you to get better. I realized that day, when I saw them, that I was truly a disgrace to myself.

There are some things in life that we may never understand. It can take days, months, or even years for one moment to finally make sense.

Write down what has happened in your life that you still do not understand why it happened.

_____

_____

_____

_____

_____

_____

_____

_____

My attackers were never caught. Everyone has a story about what they "heard" happened to me. I have been told that I was jumped by six guys. I was also told that I was attacked by just one person. I also heard that I was hit in the head with a crowbar. Honestly, I do not know what happened and I could not recall if I tried.

18

That day is forever lost, but never forgotten. All I know is that, in that hospital, my life changed.

When I woke up from the coma, I saw it. It was clear, and it was bright, yet subtle. I saw the white light! It was beautiful! There, in the corner of the hospital room, in that bright light, stood a man. He did not say a word. Because of the neck brace I had on, I was unable to look directly at him, but I knew what he wanted and who he was. Even though he did not say a word, I understood everything. I made a vow that day. The day I woke up out of the coma, I promised God that I would spread his word and, immediately, my eyes opened.

Chapter 2

Meeting God

My mom kept me in church, every Sunday. My best friend, Tevin and I would be the only two kids in Sunday School. Both of our mothers raised us in church.

We were on the youth usher board, custodians, stewards, and in the youth choir. I was familiar with Christ. Growing up, I was always told that I would be a pastor and that I would be a great preacher. This always made me angry because people were quick to tell me what I would be, without asking me what I wanted to be.

The main reason it had me upset was because I witnessed pastors live double lives.

But the day I met with God, face to face, I knew it was him. I could just feel his presence. It is like being surrounded with peace, clarity, but also conviction.

In the hospital, I knew Jesus was in that light. I made a vow that I would spread the message of God. I was afraid for my life, but I was also happy because I felt free.

In 2011, I said yes to my mission on Earth. It would still take me three years before I began fulfilling the vow I took.

From August 2011 to December 2011, I had over thirteen surgeries. Twelve focused on my throat and one focused on the reconstruction of my right eye. These were the roughest times of my life. Having others bathe, feed, and dress me, were humbling experiences.

I quickly realized that there is a difference between knowing of God and actually knowing God. Man, I swear my life did not get any better, it got worse.

After my final surgery, I decided it was best for me to return to Coastal Carolina as a full-time student. One day, my professor called on me to read aloud, in class. It was difficult to read aloud because of the damages to my throat. I was out of breath before finishing a sentence. I was embarrassed. Being out of breath started to become common after any physical movement or activity. Because of this, I took a medical leave of absence that semester.

By 2012, I was better. I hit the campus of Coastal Carolina University, once again. Man, it felt good to be back. My homies were excited and, of course, we did it big. I began to cut back on partying and focused on personal development. I got a job, working in a barbershop, and everything started falling into place. Life was getting back to being great again.

I always kept the thought in my mind that I would never be hurt again. I would never let my mom and grandmother see me down and out. So, I went out and bought a 9 millimeter. It was beautiful and it went with me everywhere that I went. I carried it in the barbershops, the grocery stores, and even to classes. Literally, all I was thinking about was never being attacked again. Carrying that gun did not make me feel untouchable instead, it made me wiser. I learned to control my anger. I learned patience. Because I was always carrying, I knew there was no time for errors or arguments. Over time, I began to sell nickel and dime bags of weed. I didn't have to, I just wanted to. My second day selling weed I got caught and arrested. I was set up at the barbershop I worked in. Two undercover cops arrested me, and I was charged with unlawful carrying of a pistol and possession of marijuana. I now had a felony. The hardest part was telling my mom, on Mother's Day, that I had been arrested.

Being behind those bars for sixteen hours was more than enough to show me that I was not jail material.

Because of my felony I was kicked out of Coastal Carolina University. My life was now upside down. There was nothing that my boys, momma, or grandmother could do for me; I felt alone!

Just like many of you, there came a time in my life where I was lost. Where I felt as though I traveled from the bottom to the top, just to take a trip back to the bottom. Humility can be uneasy. So, one of two things can happen to you:

1. You can humble yourself.

2. Or God can humble you.

Choosing the latter, like I did, came at a cost. It cost me my life and over thirteen surgeries. It cost me my freedom, my education, and my manhood.

There will come a time in your life where you will have to make a decision. Will you be ready to step up to the plate and live your life to your greatest potential? Will you decide to live for God or live for man?

Write down the thing you know you need to do, that will help you live a prosperous life.

_____

_____

_____

_____

_____

_____

_____

_____

_____

_____

_____

_____

Chapter 3

I Woke Up

The greatest part about life is that you are the only person and the only thing that you take with you every place that you travel.

I moved to Washington D.C. on faith. I did not have a plan, but I just knew I needed to get away. It was a blessing that I was accepted into Howard University. Howard University transformed my life.

Mr. Bob, a friend of the family, took me to Howard's campus on a hot summer afternoon. We arrived! I could hear the instruments being played as we walked up. Mr. Bob was a volunteer video director for the Howard University's Showtime Marching Band. They were directed by Dr. John Newson. After practice, Mr. Bob sat me down, with Dr. Newson, and from that conversation I was accepted into the University, in just a few short hours. That leap of faith had paid off.

There are certain assignments, in your life, that you are called to. Based on your faith, are you fulfilling those assignments or just existing? Many people are dead before they die! I refuse. Many people do not have enough belief to believe in what they believe in. In order to succeed, you have to faith it. Faith is like a muscle. It gets stronger every time you work it. Do it, afraid!

Write down all the reasons why it is important for you to live a prosperous life.

_____

_____

_____

_____

_____

_____

_____

_____

_____

_____

_____

_____

Once again, I felt alone. I went from a University where everyone knew me, to a University where not a single person knew my name. It was depressing. It was a culture shock. Growing up in South Carolina, it was common to interact with white folks. So, I was cool with being around white folks, especially at Coastal Carolina University. Howard, on the other hand, was all Black. I did not see any other ethnicities for the first two months. I learned so much about Black people. Honestly, at 22, it was my first time meeting Black people who were from different countries. I began to fall in love with the campus. Even though I did not have friends, I was having fun. It was different. I spent afternoons and weekends traveling with the band. It was my duty to make sure the equipment and water were on the bus. In DC, I learned how to be invisible. Walking on the streets of DC, if you do not mind your business, you will become the business. I learned how to adapt to any environment.

Growing up, I loved to watch movies and I still do. At Howard, I learned how to create movies. I learned all the ins and outs of movies. It was fun and once again, I had another opportunity that I knew I had to take advantage of. By the time I graduated, I had earned a prestigious award as "one of the best audio producers" in my graduating class. It was an easy award. Why? Because I came from nothing and I understood what it meant to take advantage of my opportunities. I understood that it did not matter about anyone else. It only mattered that I performed above and beyond. People were counting on me.

With everything that you are doing in life, ask yourself a question. "Who are you doing it for?" Is it for your benefit? Or for the benefit of others around you? Howard University allowed me to give hope and vision to kids who had none. Howard gave me hope.

In high school, I toured Howard and I was afraid of the campus. I was afraid because I did not want to depart from all I knew. And for that reason, all I knew, resulted in my being on life support.

On Howard's campus there was a certain fraternity that I wanted to be a member of. The men in my life, whom I looked up to, were all members of this fraternity. My high school football coach, my uncle, and Dr. Newson. I made it known that I was interested, and they denied me. I was told that "I would never be able to become a member." But they did not know where I came from. My entire life, I had earned everything I wanted. So, if I said I was going to do something, you could believe that I was going to do it. It took me a while to become a member of this fraternity, but I did. On April 4, 2014, my line brothers and I marched across the campus of Howard University, as the newest members of The Omega Psi Phi Fraternity,

Incorporated at Alpha Chapter. It was one of the best days of my life. To see my mom, my girlfriend, (now my wife) and other family members was amazing. It was like, the more I ran away from Howard, the further I ran away from my dreams. The closer I got to that campus, the more my goals unfolded. It was a divine road to greatness.

D.C was not all peachy. During my time there, I became an alcoholic. I would get tipsy, every night, and it got to the point where I would puke just as much as I drank. I didn't feel as though I had a problem; however, Rekka (my wife) did. She walked me through the process of healing myself and seeking help. I started smoking more weed; good weed! Once again, she walked me through that process. Rekka was and still is my rock. My knight in shining armor. She loves me, unconditionally, and I her.

One of the hardest challenges for me was commitment. I knew how to mess up a good thing. I made an executive decision that I could no longer be in a long-distance relationship. But I never told Rekka, until it was too late. I started dating a girl in DC just because I could, although I knew deep down she was not the one. The day I told Rekka I could see the pain and hurt and instantly, I regretted living life. It was so painful watching the pain in her eyes.

This great guy told me, be careful that you do not fall in love with the wrong things, because the wrong thing will take you down the wrong path. In life, we tend to wonder if the grass is really greener on the other side. Do not wonder- it is not. What you have is more than enough. It is abundant. Rekka was and is everything I need in life. More than my wife, she is my best friend.

Boys play games. Boys have girls. It takes a man to have one. You decide-boy or Man!

Write down why it is important for you to be committed to one significant other.

_____

_____

_____

_____

_____

_____

_____

_____

_____

_____

Every student should have a desire for success. If you know a student who does not have a goal, then distancing yourself is highly suggested. The burning desire to take care of myself and my family has always been my motivation; it comes from within. The days of seeing my Mom and Grandma struggle did something to me. It showed me how I did not want to live my life. At my high school graduation, I remember looking into the crowd and seeing my Father. A man who was absent throughout my life, sitting there, cheering me on as if he had supported me my entire life. It created a desire of never wanting my children to experience that feeling. At the age of 26, I don't have it all together, but I am better than I used to be. I learned to ask for help; I learned that money is not a bad thing. The more money, the more opportunities you have in life. Success does not come to those who wait. It does not care about where you are from or what tragic event has happened in your life. Success is mixing all of these trials and tribulations in a melting pot and making some delicious stew. I serve as a reminder to those who gave up on themselves and their dreams. I serve as a reminder that your story, your past, and your mistakes do not control you; you control them. Use this to your advantage.

There came a time where procrastination no longer had control. A lacking mindset was no longer acceptable. I pray every day that God, the Father of Christ, guides you to the promised land.

The culture of your life depends solely on the thoughts you think from within.

Write down how this book has helped you develop a positive mindset despite your challenges.

_____

_____

_____

_____

_____

_____

_____

_____

_____

_____

_____

_____

All I ever wanted to do was be successful. I am obsessed. To have my Mother smile and to give her the opportunity to live a full life, travel the world, cook meals, and make others laugh, is everything I want for her. I dream of the day I can build her a house, that is paid in full. I dream of the days that scholarships and highways are named after me. I dream of the day I pull up in my Mercedes Benz S class. Just the thought of becoming everything I knew I would, inspires me to wake me up at 5am, every morning. It is so close to me that I can physically touch the lifestyle I imagined.

Chapter 4

Boys II Men

T.D Jakes stated, "God gives us opportunities and what we do with those opportunities are our gift(s) to God".

My definition of a man is a person who captures his highest potential and lives in that place, every day.

Your upbringing, your economy, nor your problems, define you. You are defined by the consistent actions that you take, daily, when no one is looking.

Melqaam's 3 steps to becoming a man:

1. Moment

2. Aspirations

3. Now

In this moment, you have to accept who you are. I give you permission to acknowledge your biggest failures and acknowledge your greatest achievements. If you have been raised by a woman, who did her best to teach you how to become a "man", that can be a problem. But you are the solution. At this moment, you have to make a decision. Will you take actions to chase after your dream or will you drift through another year?

A man must always keep his dreams, his goals, and his aspirations, in the forefront of his mind. Why? Because a person without a destination is a lost person. It is like driving a car to nowhere. Your GPS does not care where you are coming from, it only cares about getting you to your destination.

Now is the time where you get to work. The phrase "I don't know how" is no longer a crutch. Figure it out! If you want to be the man you were created to be, then the actions you take today will define your tomorrow.

I can only give you the blueprint of how I became a man. My struggles, my laughs, and my tears no longer have control. Take control of your life. It is time for you to get off life support and breathe on your own! Just because your dreams have not happened yet, does not mean that they are never going to happen. Stay faithful and keep dreaming.

To whom much is given, much is required.

Chapter 5

Wake Up: Your Next Chapter of Life

As I sit here thinking, listening to music, while writing to you, the greater version of you....the Highest you, I can believe, in true confidence, that you are in the midst of your journey! You are on the way. Enjoy it!

When I was on life support, I was unconscious, while subconsciously awake. When I was in the streets, living a life of violence, while creating ungodly chaos, I was "woke". I thought I knew it all. No one could give me advice. I was woke!

Many of you are currently living a life that is not producing happiness. Your soul is empty. You feel the void of a life with no purpose, so you continue to self-sabotage. You, too, are a "know-it-all." And you believe that you are "woke".

It was when I heard the doctor say, "Mr. Shaw, you are in the ICU at Grand Strand Hospital, in Myrtle Beach, SC. You are on life support.", that I (the greater me) was awakened, even though I was still unconscious!

When are you going to wake up?

Core 15

1. Self confidence

When you start seeing your worth, you'll find it harder to stay around people who don't . *Unknown*

Talk to yourself like you would to someone you love. *Brene Brown*

When your past tries to confront you, remember why you left it behind. *Julien Oglesby*

2. Academic Confidence

Do you truly believe in yourself? If so, then why do your grades look the way that they do?! *Melqaam Shaw*

The vision is so clear you can see it in HD. *Tara Kirkpatrick*

If you think education is expensive, try ignorance. *Andy McIntye*

3. Academic Probation

Continue your quest for success. Your academic journey doesn't end here. *Melqaam Shaw*

Take responsibility and change the situation. *Melqaam Shaw*

You cannot give up, in this season. *Melqaam Shaw*

4. Upbringing

Live from the 843... South Carolina Stand Up. *Melqaam Shaw*

Focus more on who you were created to be. *Unknown*

Pretty much all the honest truth telling there is in the world, is done by children. *Unknown*

5. Family Values

When all the dust is settled and all the crowds are gone, the things that matter are faith, family, and friends. *Barbara Bush*

Value not the things you have in life, but rather who you have in life. *Unknown*

Family is one of nature's masterpieces. *George Santayana*

6. Self-Ignorance

Some of y'all are woke but not awake.
Melqaam Shaw

Don't be who you want to be. Be who
you are called to be. *Melqaam Shaw*

A man who does not read, is a poor
man. *Unknown*

7. Communicating With Your Educator

The single biggest problem in communication is the illusion that it has taken place. *George Bernard Shaw*

Educating the mind, without educating the heart, is no education at all. *Aristotle*

8. Lack of Academic Preparation

Don't pay for validation, pay for phenomenal coaching. *Melqaam Shaw*

I can't help you if you do not help yourself. *My Grandma*

9. Don't Understand Material

Don't let what you cannot do interfere with what you can do . *John Wooden*

10. Work Ethic

Strive for progress, not perfection.
Unknown

Success is to be measured, not so
much by the position that one has
reached in life, as by the obstacles
which he has overcome while trying to
succeed. *Booker T Washington*

11. Social Activities

Don't travel for Instagram, travel for purpose. *Melqaam Shaw*

12. Campus Resources

Education is the most powerful weapon you can use to change the world. *Nelson Mandela*

13. Transition From High School to College

You are only facing what others have met. *Will Dromgoole*

14. Study Skills

If you study to remember, you will forget, but if you study to understand, you will remember. *Unknown*

15. Leave The Streets Alone

If your purpose is a check then you might want to check your purpose. *Trey Chaplin*

You are going to keep thinking you are about that life until a machine is saving your life. *Melqaam Shaw*

For more information on working with Melqaam Shaw or hosting him at your next event, simply contact:

MelqaamShaw.com

CPSIA information can be obtained
at www.ICGtesting.com
Printed in the USA
FSHW020805081020
74519FS

9 781087 879864